30 Days of Sex Talks
Empowering Your Child with Knowledge of Sexual Intimacy
Ages 8-11

Rising Parent Media, LLC

20 19 18 17 16   2 3 4

ISBN: 978-0-9863708-1-6 (paperback)

www.educateempowerkids.org

30 DAYS OF SEX TALKS

FOR 8–11
YEAR-OLDS

EMPOWERING YOUR CHILD WITH
KNOWLEDGE OF SEXUAL INTIMACY

BY
EDUCATE AND EMPOWER KIDS

FOR GREAT RESOURCES AND INFORMATION, FOLLOW US:

Facebook: www.facebook.com/educateempowerkids/
Twitter: @EduEmpowerKids
Pinterest: pinterest.com/educateempower/
Instagram: Eduempowerkids

EDUCATE AND EMPOWER KIDS WOULD LIKE TO ACKNOWLEDGE
THE FOLLOWING PEOPLE WHO CONTRIBUTED TIME,TALENTS,
AND ENERGY TO THIS PUBLICATION:

Dina Alexander, MS
Amanda Scott
Jenny Webb, MA
Caron C. Andrews

Ed Allison
Mary Ann Benson, MSW, LSW
Scott Hounsell
Cliff Park, MBA

DESIGN AND ILLUSTRATION BY:
Jera Mehrdad

30 DAYS OF SEX TALKS
TABLE OF CONTENTS

INTRODUCTION

Sexual intimacy is one of the greatest experiences available to us as human beings. We feel that it is imperative that you are able to clearly express this sentiment to your child. Each of us at Educate and Empower Kids is a parent and like all parents, we feel charged with providing positive, thought-provoking experiences for our children to learn from. In the world we live in, this is not an easy task. Our goal is not only to provide you with an opportunity to start conversations about crucial topics, but also to help you create an environment in your home which encourages open discussions about the many other issues which will inevitably come up as you are raising your child. Talking with your child about sex and intimacy is a great way to open the door for other important discussions. After all, this is what makes us human—it's part of what makes the human experience beautiful.

It is within this age group that children become much more aware of their bodies. Knowledge about how the human body works, how your child's body is going to change and how he or she can be ready for these things can empower your child. This age is also when children begin to have feelings of being attracted to others. This is why it's important to discuss relationships, gender and pornography as well. If you feel like your child isn't mature enough to address the bullets provided, you may want to purchase the curriculum we have developed for the 3-7 year old age group as a starting point.

The purpose of this curriculum is to help you as parents establish and grow open and honest communication with your child about sex, intimacy, the dangers of online pornography and your child's view of him or herself. We believe that once you have started these conversations, you will be empowered to talk to your child about anything.

Our mission is to empower families to create deep, meaningful connection. Children in the US spend an average of 7.5 hours consuming media each day (Boyse, RN, 2010). Additionally, according to one study, 42% of children had been exposed to pornography in the past year and of those, 67% were exposed to it accidentally (Wolack, et al., 2007). With the amount of sex and violence in almost every medium our kids are watching, we need to ask ourselves what we are doing to counteract all that screen time.

With this program, we've made it simple for you to talk about the beauty of love, sex, bodies and relationships. You can discuss sex in the context in which it belongs; as a part of a healthy relationship that also includes joy, laughter and the full range of emotion that defines human intimacy.

It's imperative that you begin your daily talks with just one topic in mind and that you make every experience, however brief, truly meaningful.

GETTINGSTARTED

The curriculum includes a book, glossary and a code to download the topic cards. Each topic is followed by several bullet points. These bullet points contain terms to define and discuss with your child as well as questions or statements designed to inspire conversations between you and your child. We've included definitions, sample dialogue and even some activities to make it simple and to help you get started. If you feel like your child isn't ready to discuss the bullets listed under the topic or if you feel that your child's knowledge is more advanced, please note that we have also developed this curriculum for other age groups and it is available for purchase. It's important to discuss things with your child based on his or her own maturity level; progressing or referring back at your own pace.

The hard work has all been done for you, you need not be an expert. In fact, we feel strongly that leaning on your own personal experiences—both mistakes and successes—is a great way to use life lessons to teach your child. If done properly, these talks will bring you closer to your child than you ever could have imagined. You know and love your child more than anyone, so you decide when and where these discussions take place. In time, you will recognize and enjoy teaching moments in everyday life with your child.

Early in the research for this curriculum, our Vice President had an experience while shopping with her children. As she passed a mall lingerie store with her two young sons, she decided to seize the moment and explain to her boys about body image, photo manipulation and unrealistic portrayals of people in advertising. Soon, you too will recognize and take advantage of moments like these in your own life and your child will be better informed and more prepared because of them. Because the truth is that your child will be exposed to hyper-sexualized media eventually, you need to give him or her the framework to be ready and convey to your child what healthy sexuality really is.

This book works well with the downloadable topic cards (online code is available in the back of the book). On the following pages you'll find each topic with its bullet points listed, followed by ideas for further discussion items, questions you may want to ask, and points to consider when talking with your child about that topic. Throughout the book we've also included several suggested scenarios that you could pose to your child to prompt additional thoughts and discussions of specific situations that could arise in his or her life.

As you work through the topics, think about sharing your ideas and your personal or family standards; encouraging your child to share their thoughts and feelings. Talk about both the emotional and physical aspects of each topic and discuss emotional and physical safety. Be sure to ask your child questions to help draw him or her out. *These topics are starting points.* If additional or different conversations arise, follow them. This curriculum is designed to be personalized to you and your child. Consistent conversation is the key to successfully implementing this program. Remember, the goal is not only to present useful information to your child, but to normalize the process of talking to each other about these topics.

We strongly encourage you to read through the suggested topics, bullet points, and ideas in the parent book before talking with your child. Here are a few tips:

- Plan ahead of time but don't create an event. Having a plan or planning ahead of time will remove much of the awkwardness you might feel in talking about these subjects with your child. In not creating an event, you are making the discussions feel more spontaneous, the experience more repeatable and yourself more approachable.

- Consider your individual child's age, developmental stage, and personality in conjunction with each topic, as well as your family's values and individual situation, and adapt the material in order to produce the best discussion.

There are additional resources listed in the back of the book as well as a glossary to help you define the terms used.

INSTRUCTIONS

BE THE SOURCE

You direct the conversations. Bring up issues that you feel are most important and allow the conversation to flow from there. You love and know your child better than anyone else, so you are the best person to judge what will be most effective: Taking into account personal values, religious beliefs, individual personalities, and family dynamics. Our goal is to provide you with a simple structure and guide for how to introduce and discuss a variety of topics. We want to help you, the parent, be the best source of information about sex and intimacy for your child. If you don't discuss these topics, your child will look for answers from other, less reliable *and sometimes dangerous* sources like: the internet, the media, and other kids.

FOCUS ON INTIMACY

Help your child understand how incredible and uniting sex can be. Don't just focus on the mechanics, spend a significant amount of time talking about the beauty of love and sex, the reality of real relationships and how they are built and maintained. Children are constantly exposed to unhealthy examples of relationships in the media. Many of them are teaching your child lessons about sexuality and interactions between people that are misleading, incomplete, and unhealthy. Real emotional intimacy is rarely portrayed, so it's your job to model positive behavior. You can help your child connect the dots between healthy relationships and healthy sexuality when you model positive ways for your child to like and care for his or her body; to protect, have a positive attitude toward and make favorable choices for that body.

ANSWER YOUR CHILD'S QUESTIONS

If you are embarrassed by your child's curiosity and questions, you imply that there is something shameful about these topics. However, if you answer your child's questions openly and honestly, you demonstrate that sexuality is positive and healthy relationships are something to seek when the time is right. Answer your child's questions honestly and openly and your child will learn that you are available not just for *this* discussion, but for *any* discussion. It's okay if you don't have all the answers. Tell your child you will find out for him or her; because it's better that you go searching instead of your child doing so. See the resources at the end of this book and on our resources page at www.educateempowerkids.org for further information on these and other topics.

BEPOSITIVE

Take the fear and shame out of these discussions. Sex is natural and wondrous and your child should feel nothing but positivity about it from you. If you do feel awkward, stay calm and use matter-of-fact tones and discussion. It's easier than you think- just open your mouth and begin! *It will get easier with every talk you have with your child.* After a couple of talks, he or she will begin to look forward to this time that you are spending together and so will you. Taking the time to talk about these things will reiterate to your child how important he or she is to you. Use experiences from your own life to begin a discussion if it makes you feel more comfortable. We have listed some tough topics here, but they are all discussed in a positive, informative way. Don't worry, we are with you every step of the way!

NEEDTOKNOW

• This curriculum is not a one-size-fits all. *You* guide the conversation and lead the discussion according to your unique situation.

• No program can cover all aspects of sexual intimacy perfectly for every individual circumstance. You can empower yourself with the knowledge you gain from this program to share with your child what you feel is the most important.

• This program is meant to be simple! It's organized into simple topics with bullet points to be straightforward and create conversations.

FINALLY

This program is meant to inspire conversations that we hope assist you in fostering an environment where difficult discussions are made easier. The hope is that your child will feel like he or she can talk to you about anything. This program is a great tool that your kids will look forward to! Take advantage of the one on one time that these discussions facilitate to become more comfortable talking with your child.

It's recommended that you designate with your child and within your home a "safe zone," meaning that during the course of these conversations, your child should feel free and safe to ask any questions and make any comments without judgment or repercussion. Your child should be able to use the term "safe zone" again and again to discuss, confide and consult with you about the tough subjects he or she will be confronted with throughout life.

It's highly recommended that, whenever possible, all parenting parties be involved in these discussions.

Citations
Boyse, RN, K. (2010, August 1). Television (TV) and Children. Retrieved November 13, 2014, from http://www.med.umich.edu/yourchild/topics/tv.htm

Wolack, et al. (2007, February 2). Unwanted and Wanted Exposure to Online Pornography in a National Sample of Youth Internet Users. Retrieved November 13, 2014, from http://pediatrics.aappublications.org/content/119/2/247.full

LET'S GET STARTED!

AGES
8-11

It is within this age group that children become much more aware of their bodies. Knowledge about how the human body works, how your child's body is going to change and how he or she can be ready for these things can empower your child.

This age is also when children begin to have feelings of being attracted to others. This is why it's important to discuss relationships, gender, and pornography as well. If you feel like your child isn't mature enough to address the bullets provided, you may want to refer back to the 3-7 age group curriculum as a starting point for those particular discussions.

PUBLIC: *Belonging to or for the use of all people in a specific area, or all people as a whole. Something that is public is common, shared, collective, communal, and widespread.*

START THE CONVERSATION

Parents discuss things with their children at different ages. Remind your child that his or her siblings may not be ready to know the information you are entrusting him or her with. Remind your child that his or her friends may not be ready to discuss topics like sex and puberty and that those topics should only be discussed with parents, to avoid confusion. Give reasons for these topics being private: small children are not ready to hear about it, some people are uncomfortable talking about sex and sex shouldn't be discussed amongst children.

ADDITIONAL QUESTIONS TO CONSIDER

What are things we can talk about in public with our friends?

When is a good time to have a private discussion?

Who are some good people to ask private questions to?

Have you and your friends ever talked about sex?

Why is it not a good idea to talk to my friends about sex?

1.
PUBLIC VS PRIVATE

- WHY ARE SOME TOPICS PRIVATE?

- I CAN ASK MY PARENTS DIFFICULT QUESTIONS

- MY HOME IS A SAFE ZONE

- IS IT OKAY FOR AN ADULT OTHER THAN YOUR PARENTS TO DISCUSS SEX WITH YOU?

SAMPLE SCENARIO

Consider describing some ways myths about sex, body parts and other private topics can be spread when misinformed people discuss them. Some myths might include: masturbating will make one blind, a woman can't get pregnant while she is having her period, or eating certain foods makes one amorous.

2.
MALE
ANATOMY

- PENIS
- TESTICLE/SCROTUM
- ANUS

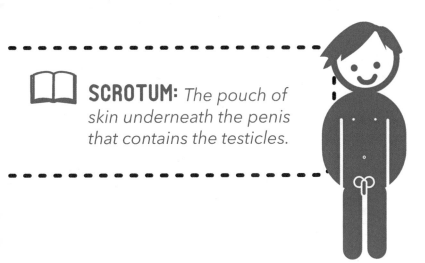

SCROTUM: *The pouch of skin underneath the penis that contains the testicles.*

START THE CONVERSATION

Communicate that sexual organs are the most fundamental way that boys are different from girls. Refer to the way a doctor determines the sex of a baby by a visual inspection. Explain how the penis and scrotum can expand and contract with body temperature. If you have a diagram, now may be a good time to use it. Talk about the breasts, nipples and how, even in men, they can be tender. Describe how nipples can be many shapes, sizes and colors. Asking your child if he or she has heard any slang terms is a good way to gauge if he or she has been talking about or hearing about sex outside your home.

What are some things that make boys and girls physically different? What are some things that make us the same?

ADDITIONAL QUESTIONS TO CONSIDER

We have talked about the medically correct terms for these body parts but there are many slang terms as well. What are some you have heard?

What questions do you have about your body?

3.
FEMALE ANATOMY

- 💬 VAGINA
- 💬 URETHRA
- 💬 ANUS
- 💬 BREASTS/NIPPLES
- 💬 VULVA

VULVA: *The parts of the female sexual organs that are on the outside of the body.*

START THE CONVERSATION

Communicate that sexual organs are the most fundamental way that boys are different from girls. Refer to the way a doctor determines the sex of a baby by a visual inspection. Explain the many parts of the vagina and their uses. If you have a diagram, now may be a good time to use it. If you are discussing this topic with your daughter, you may even want to encourage her to look at her vagina in a mirror.

Describe how the anus is located in the same general area but is completely different from the vagina and is not a sexual organ. Talk about the uses of breasts and nipples. Describe how they can be many shapes, sizes and colors. Asking your child if he or she has heard any slang terms is a good way to gauge if he or she has been talking about or hearing about sex outside your home. Explain the many parts and uses of the vagina. See glossary for additional definitions.

ADDITIONAL QUESTIONS TO CONSIDER

We have talked about the medically correct terms for these body parts but there are many slang terms as well. What are some you have heard?

What are some things that make boys and girls physically different? What are some things that make us the same?

Every part of your body is special and worth protecting. Why do you think yours is worth protecting?

START THE CONVERSATION

Describe how boys begin to grow hair under their arms, in the pubic area, and with thicker growth in places like legs and arms and chest. Sweat glands will produce more, and the area under the arms might smell unpleasant. The nipple and breast area may become tender and swell a bit. The voice will begin to deepen and, as a result, may "crack" occasionally. Touch on how emotional and sensitive boys can become during this time due to hormonal changes. If you are discussing this with your son and he is ready, you might want to discuss feelings of arousal and explain that his body's reactions are completely normal and nothing to feel ashamed of. Talk about ways to handle "spontaneous erections" in public situations. Nocturnal emissions or "wet dreams" are a common occurrence at this age and nothing to be embarrassed about or feel ashamed of.

Puberty is a great time for kids to learn how to use the washing machine because of the sweaty clothes and sheets. Don't forget to mention that frequent (if not daily!) showering will become a must during this time period. Mention that it helps every guy look and feel better. Talk about the amazing things the male body can do!

ADDITIONAL QUESTIONS TO CONSIDER

Have you noticed any changes in your body? Are there any changes in your body that you are looking forward to? Is there anything about puberty you're confused about?

What's the most exciting thing about growing up?

Have you noticed other kids your age starting to change? How would you feel if you didn't hit puberty at the same time your friends did?

SAMPLE DIALOGUE

If possible, talk about Dad's age when he began puberty. Talk about how this is sometimes an indicator of when a son will begin. Share your experience.

4.
PUBERTY FOR BOYS

- **PHYSICAL CHANGES: HAIR GROWTH, SWEAT, VOICE CHANGES**

- **EMOTIONAL CHANGES**

- **NOCTURNAL EMISSIONS (OR "WET DREAMS")**

- **SPONTANEOUS ERECTION**

 NOCTURNAL EMISSIONS:
A spontaneous orgasm that occurs during sleep.

5. PUBERTY FOR GIRLS

- PHYSICAL CHANGES: HAIR GROWTH, SWEAT, BREAST DEVELOPMENT

- EMOTIONAL CHANGES

- FEELINGS OF AROUSAL, WETNESS AND DISCHARGE IN VAGINAL AREA ARE NORMAL

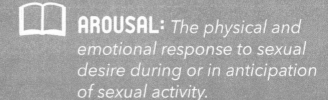 **AROUSAL:** *The physical and emotional response to sexual desire during or in anticipation of sexual activity.*

START THE CONVERSATION

Describe how girls begin to grow hair under their arms, in the pubic area, and with thicker growth in places like legs and arms. Sweat glands will produce more, and the area under the arms might smell unpleasant. Breasts will become tender and start to develop. Point out that breast development can vary widely in girls and is usually the signal of the onset of puberty. Discuss how emotional and sensitive girls can become during this time due to hormonal changes. If you are discussing this with your daughter and she is ready, you might want to discuss feelings of arousal and explain that her body's reactions are completely normal and nothing to feel ashamed of.

Puberty is a great time to discuss with your daughter the necessity of purchasing bras and picking out deodorant. You may want to teach her how to shave her legs and under arms as well.Don't forget to mention that frequent (if not daily!) showering will become a must during this time period. Mention that it helps every girl look and feel better.

Be sure to talk about the amazing things the female body can do!

ADDITIONAL QUESTIONS TO CONSIDER

Have you noticed any changes in your body? Are there any changes in your body that you are looking forward to? Is there anything about puberty you're confused about?

Growing up can be fun and challenging. How do you picture it?

Have you talked to any of your friends about these changes? What have you learned?

Is there anything I can do to help you feel more comfortable talking about these changes?

SAMPLE DIALOGUE

If possible, talk about how old Mom was when she started puberty. Talk about how this is sometimes an indicator of when a daughter will start. Share your experience.

START THE CONVERSATION

If you have a diagram, now may be a good time to use it. Explanation of menstruation: Egg is released from ovaries through fallopian tube into uterus. Each month, blood and tissue build up in the uterus. When the egg is not fertilized, this blood and tissue are not needed and are shed from the body through the vagina. A cycle is roughly 28 days but can vary. Bleeding time lasts from 2-7 days. May be accompanied by cramping, breast tenderness, and emotional sensitivity. Point out that there is no way of knowing just by looking at a girl if she is menstruating. Being prepared is a young girl's best bet! Discuss the various forms of "protection": sanitary napkins or "pads", tampons (various kinds of applicators and absorbency levels), and menstrual cups. Explain how each is used. Mention mood changes that can occur around period time, and how different girls react differently to changing hormone levels. If you are discussing this with your son, help him to understand that girls may be sensitive or embarrassed by their periods. See glossary for full definition of the Menstrual Cycle.

ADDITIONAL QUESTIONS TO CONSIDER

What have you heard about menstrual periods?

How do you feel about getting your period?

How can a girl be prepared for her period?

How can people show more sensitivity to a girl during her period?

SAMPLE DIALOGUE

If possible, talk about Mom's age when she experienced her first period. Talk about how this is sometimes an indicator of when a daughter will get her first period. Share your experience.

6.
MENSTRUAL CYCLE

- AGE OF FIRST MENSTRUATION VARIES WIDELY, AVERAGE AGE IS 12

- EGG IS RELEASED MONTHLY

- DISCHARGE (MUCUS FROM VAGINA) MAY BEGIN ABOUT 6 MONTHS BEFORE FIRST PERIOD

 MENSTRUAL PERIOD: *A discharging of blood, secretions, and tissue debris from the uterus at periods of approximately one month in females of breeding age that are not pregnant.*

7.
PHYSICAL MECHANICS OF SEXUAL INTERCOURSE

- ERECTION

- FEELINGS OF AROUSAL IN THE CLITORIS AND WETNESS IN THE VAGINAL AREA

- PENIS IS INSERTED INTO VAGINA

- SPERM IS RELEASED FROM PENIS

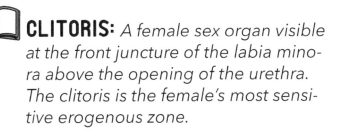

CLITORIS: *A female sex organ visible at the front juncture of the labia minora above the opening of the urethra. The clitoris is the female's most sensitive erogenous zone.*

START THE CONVERSATION

Allow your child to guide this conversation so you might know how much information he or she is ready for. Start off by asking your child what he knows about the word "sex". Use your instincts to gauge how much information he is ready for. If your child seems ready (he mentions that kids have been talking about sex on the playground or she is asking more specific questions), start with the basics and speak in the abstract. "A man and a woman each have body parts that fit together..." Your child will sense if you're uncomfortable, so try to relax! Talk about it matter-of-factly, like you would explain anything to your child!

ADDITIONAL QUESTIONS TO CONSIDER

Are your classmates talking about sex? How does that make you feel? What do you believe about it?

Why should we not just have sex with anyone? When is it ok to have sex with someone?

SAMPLE DIALOGUE

Start off by letting your child know that talking about sex can be uncomfortable or awkward for some families. And that feeling awkward is okay. Remind them that you are there to answer their questions. The bodies of men and women are designed to come together...

INTIMACY: *Generally a feeling or form of significant closeness. (See glossary for more complete definition).*

START THE CONVERSATION

Help your child to understand the connection between emotions and physical expression such as: laughing when we think something is funny, stamping a foot when we feel angry, running up to hug someone when we feel grateful, wanting a hug when we feel sad. Talk about why we only kiss people we like or love. Remind them of the good feelings we get from hugs. Explain when he or she is ready that these are the same reasons sex is better in a committed relationship. Reiterate the fact that children are not emotionally ready to have sex. Discuss your own family and personal values and beliefs about when and with whom it is appropriate to have sex.

ADDITIONAL QUESTIONS TO CONSIDER

What does "emotional intimacy" feel like? (warmth, happiness, peace, caring, etc.)

Why does loving someone make people want to express that love in a physical way?

Do you know what commitment is? Why is it good to wait to have sex until you are in a committed relationship?

Do you know why sex is an amazing and bonding experience?

8.
EMOTIONAL ASPECTS OF SEX

- **SEX CAN BE A NATURAL EXPRESSION OF EMOTIONAL LOVE**

- **CAN CREATE FEELINGS OF CONFUSION AND HURT IF NOT ACCOMPANIED BY LOVE**

- **SEX CAN BE A BINDING FORCE IN A RELATIONSHIP**

9.
RELATIONSHIPS ARE GOOD AND WONDERFUL

- WHAT IS A RELATIONSHIP?

- EMOTIONAL AND SPIRITUAL BENEFITS OF MONOGAMY

- HEALTH BENEFITS OF MONOGAMY

MONOGAMY:
A relationship in which a person has one partner at any one time.

START THE CONVERSATION

There is no perfect indicator of readiness for a relationship, but age, maturity level, personal responsibility and accountability are good indicators of readiness. Discuss your personal opinion on this subject. Monogamy is a sexual relationship between two people, excluding all others. Talk about the emotional benefits (connectedness) and health benefits (less risk of STIs).

This is a great time to discuss how relationships are formed and how they progress over time. You may want to share how you met your child's father/mother.

ADDITIONAL QUESTIONS TO CONSIDER

What is great about being in a relationship?

How do relationships begin?

What characteristics make a good partner?

What are the unique things you could bring to a relationship?

EMOTIONAL ABUSE: *A form of abuse in which another person is subjected to behavior that can result in psychological trauma. (See glossary for more definitions of abuse.)*

START THE CONVERSATION
Help your child understand that both parties in any relationship are equal. Neither person is above the other and no one, no matter what they have done, deserves to be abused by another person. Do you know what abuse looks like?

ADDITIONAL QUESTIONS TO CONSIDER
What do you think are the differences between a healthy relationship and an abusive one?

What adults do you know that have a healthy relationship?

Why is important for people in any type of relationship to treat one another with respect?

10.
WHAT DOES A HEALTHY RELATIONSHIP LOOK LIKE?

- A HEALTHY RELATIONSHIP INCLUDES GOOD COMMUNICATION

- IT IS NOT OKAY TO PHYSICALLY HURT ANOTHER PERSON

- ABUSE CAN BE EMOTIONAL, MENTAL, AND/OR PHYSICAL

- BOTH PEOPLE IN A RELATIONSHIP DESERVE RESPECT AND DIGNITY

SURVEY 1 8-11

Please reflect on your discussions with your child up to this point and answer the following questions.

1. Select the topic that has provided the best discussion with your child thus far.

   1. Public versus Private Discussion
   2. Male Anatomy
   3. Female Anatomy
   4. Puberty for Boys
   5. Puberty for Girls
   6. Menstrual Cycle
   7. Physical Mechanics of Sexual Intercourse
   8. Emotional Aspects of Sex
   9. Relationships are Good and Wonderful
   10. What Does a Healthy Relationship Look Like?

2. Referring to question 1, please describe what made this your best discussion.

   _____

   _____

3. Referring to question 1, were there things that you did during your discussion that were different from other discussions? If so, what were they and can you replicate them?

   _____

   _____

4. What has your child said that surprised you during your first 10 discussions?

_____

_____

5. If you have any additional comments, please write them here:

_____

_____

If you scan the code below, you can take this survey online. This will help us improve our curriculum and create new resources for parents.

11.
ROMANTIC LOVE

- WHAT DO YOU THINK ROMANTIC LOVE IS?

- HOW IS THIS DIFFERENT FROM OTHER KINDS OF LOVE?

- HOW DO PEOPLE SHOW ROMANTIC LOVE?

- WHAT DO YOU THINK FALLING IN LOVE FEELS LIKE?

START THE CONVERSATION

Explain that romantic love is different from physical attraction. Describe how a person can be physically attracted to another without falling in love. Tell your child it is normal to love friends and want to spend time together. Give examples of how people express romantic love: for example, kissing, dating, staring into each other's eyes, etc. Describe what romantic love means to you. Discuss romantic love as something that happens between older people.

ADDITIONAL QUESTIONS TO CONSIDER

Who do we know that has a romantic relationship? How can you tell?

How will you know you're ready to be in a romantic relationship?

 ROMANTIC LOVE:
A form of love that denotes intimacy and a strong desire for emotional connection with another person to whom one is generally also sexually attracted.

12.
DIFFERENT KINDS OF FAMILIES

- THERE ARE MANY DIFFERENT KINDS OF FAMILIES

- SOME KIDS ARE RAISED BY GRANDPARENTS, AUNTS AND UNCLES, OR OTHER FAMILY MEMBERS

- SOME KIDS ARE RAISED BY A SINGLE PARENT

- SOME KIDS ARE RAISED BY TWO DADS OR TWO MOMS

- SOME KIDS ARE RAISED BY ONE MOM AND ONE DAD

FAMILY: *A group consisting of parents and children living together in a household. (See glossary for further definition.)*

START THE CONVERSATION

Every family is different and special in its own way. It is important that we love our friends and those we interact with regardless of their family circumstance. Emphasize that family is important, and we should not put down our friends because their family is different than ours.

ADDITIONAL QUESTIONS TO CONSIDER

How would you describe your family?

Who do we know who has a family that is different than ours?

Tell me what you imagine your future family will be like? Do you want it to be like our family?

GENDER ROLE:
The pattern of masculine or feminine behavior of an individual that is defined by a particular culture and that is largely determined by a child's upbringing.

START THE CONVERSATION

Encourage a good conversation about stereotyping and typical male and female roles. Explain that although our bodies are different in fundamental ways, women and men can perform the same tasks equally well. Share your personal thoughts.

ADDITIONAL QUESTIONS TO CONSIDER

Is it okay for boys to be interested in what are thought of as feminine things and for girls to be interested in typically masculine things?

Why is it important to look past a friend's likes, and instead focus on who they are?

13.
GENDER ROLES

- ARE THERE TYPICAL BOY AND GIRL INTERESTS?

- IT'S OKAY FOR BOYS AND GIRLS TO PURSUE WHATEVER ACTIVITIES THEY ARE INTERESTED IN DOING

- DON'T LET STEREO-TYPICAL GENDER ROLES STOP YOU FROM TRYING SOMETHING NEW

14.
SEXUAL IDENTIFICATION

- IT IS INDIVIDUAL AND UNIQUE

- LOVING YOUR FRIENDS IS DIFFERENT FROM BEING "IN LOVE"

- YOUR SEXUALITY IS AN INTEGRAL PART OF YOU BUT IT DOES NOT DEFINE WHO YOU ARE

- BE CAREFUL TO NOT HAVE YOUR SEXUALITY DEFINED FOR YOU BY OUTSIDE INFLUENCES (FRIENDS, MEDIA, ETC.)

START THE CONVERSATION

Talk with your child about the many different kinds of sexual identifications. Discuss heterosexual, gay, lesbian, bisexual, transgender, intersex, and asexual sexual identifications. Describe how identifying oneself as any of these does not strictly define a person. Explain the difference between friend love and sexual attraction. Make it clear that liking someone or being a fan of someone who is gay (a friend or on TV) does not make someone gay. No one's sexuality should be influenced by anyone or anything else. Ask your child what his or her thoughts are on the subject. Reiterate that we should never mistreat people for being different. Share your personal/family thoughts and thoughts and understanding of the topic.

ADDITIONAL QUESTIONS TO CONSIDER

What does LGBTQI stand for?

What does it mean to be gay?

How are gay people and straight people different?

How do those who identify as gay (or any of the other terms listed above) not differ from others at all?

 ## SEXUAL IDENTIFICATION:
How one thinks of oneself in terms of whom one is romantically or sexually attracted to.

RELATIONSHIP: *The state of being connected, united, or related to another person.*

START THE CONVERSATION

Discuss the natural physical progression of a HEALTHY sexual relationship. Explain that a healthy sexual relationship is one in which both parties feel equally respected. Talk about how many healthy sexual relationships start off as friendships and begin with smaller acts of sexual intimacy (kissing, hugging, cuddling) before moving on to more intimate acts like sexual intercourse. Explain that being ready for this progression depends on age, maturity level, personal responsibility, and accountability. Reiterate your personal or family standards on this subject.

ADDITIONAL QUESTIONS TO CONSIDER

What age do you think it is okay to start having sex? Is there a right age for everyone?

What factors should be considered to determine if someone is ready for sex?

Someday you will be dating. What can you do if someone is pressuring you to have sex and you do not want to?

15.
AT WHAT AGE IS SOMEONE READY FOR A SEXUAL RELATIONSHIP?

- ● STAGES OF A PHYSICAL RELATIONSHIP: HANDHOLDING, HUGGING, KISSING, PETTING, SEX

- ● PEOPLE ARE READY FOR THESE STAGES AT DIFFERENT AGES

- ● CHILDREN ARE NOT PHYSICALLY OR EMOTIONALLY READY FOR A SEXUAL RELATIONSHIP

16.
CURIOSITY

- CURIOSITY ABOUT SEX, YOUR DEVELOPING BODY AND OTHER'S BODIES IS COMPLETELY NORMAL

- CHILDREN SHOULD NEVER FEEL ASHAMED FOR BEING CURIOUS

- IT'S IMPORTANT TO KNOW WHO TO TALK TO ABOUT YOUR CURIOSITY AND QUESTIONS

- PARENTS ARE THE BEST SOURCE OF INFORMATION AND WON'T MAKE YOU FEEL ASHAMED

START THE CONVERSATION

It's so important that children never be made to feel embarrassed for being curious. It's completely natural. Validate your child's awareness and answer questions honestly and completely. Make him or her feel as comfortable as possible when he or she comes to you with questions. Remind him or her that your home is a safe zone where questions are always okay. If some topics are too awkward to ask questions face to face, give kids the option to write it down.

ADDITIONAL QUESTIONS TO CONSIDER

What are some things about your body that you are curious about?

What else are you curious about? Would you like to know more about (pick your own topic) ...?

What can I do to help you feel more comfortable coming to me with questions?

SAMPLE DIALOGUE

Share an experience with your child about a time you were curious about something.

 CURIOSITY:
The desire to learn or know more about something or someone.

ORGASM: *The rhythmic muscular contractions in the pelvic region that occur as a result of sexual stimulation, arousal, and activity during the sexual response cycle. Orgasms are characterized by a sudden release of built-up sexual tension and by the resulting sexual pleasure.*

START THE CONVERSATION

Everyone has different opinions when it comes to masturbation. Even though (medically) the behavior can be a normal part of a child's development, for some, there are other reasons parents may wish to discourage masturbation. Discuss your personal views with your child about masturbation. Discuss privacy and appropriate times, places, etc. Discuss the possibility of addiction. However you choose to talk about masturbation with your child, it is important to let them know that they are loved.

Discuss the impulses kids start feeling around puberty and how normal and natural those feelings are. Talk about healthy ways they can handle those impulses.

If you feel your child is ready, discuss the following questions: Is it healthy to explore our bodies? What is the difference between masturbating and exploring?

Is masturbation good? Bad? Neither?

ADDITIONAL QUESTIONS TO CONSIDER

What is an appropriate time and place for masturbation?

What happens if masturbation becomes a habit?

17.
MASTURBATION

- MASTURBATION IS SELF-STIMULATION OF THE GENITALS

- SOME PEOPLE DO IT TO ACHIEVE ORGASM

- IS IT OKAY FOR KIDS?

18.
CHILDREN
DO NOT
HAVE SEX

- CHILDREN'S BODIES ARE NOT READY FOR SEX

- CHILDREN ARE NOT EMOTIONALLY READY FOR SEX

- YOU ALWAYS HAVE THE RIGHT TO SAY "NO!"

START THE CONVERSATION

An adult you can trust will never say it is normal for a child to have sex. Children's bodies are not physically mature and ready for sex. Children also have a different emotional capability than adults. These are reasons why children DO NOT have sex. It is against the law for someone to have sex with a child.

ADDITIONAL QUESTIONS TO CONSIDER

What should you do if someone tells you that sex is normal for children? Why do you think someone would say that?

What should you do if someone asks you to have sex or tries to touch the private parts of your body? Has this ever happened to you?

What should you do if a friend tells you they are being sexually abused by someone? Who can you talk to?

CHILD: *A person between birth and full growth.*

UNCOMFORTABLE: *Feeling or causing discomfort or unease; disquieting.*

START THE CONVERSATION

Make sure your child understands that he or she is NOT in trouble and why it is important to tell a trusted adult. It's important to look for physical cues here. Inform your child that it's important to tell right away, but also that it's never too late. Give reassurance that he or she will always be believed.

Talk about adults in your child's life who you trust. Ask your child to list a few people whom he or she trusts. Confirm or correct the people on this list. Remind your child that sometimes kids, touch or abuse other kids. Discuss with your child what can be done in these circumstances.

ADDITIONAL QUESTIONS TO CONSIDER

Has anyone ever touched you, talked to you, or shown you something sexual that made you feel uncomfortable?

What would you do if this happened to you?

Who are adults we can trust? Is there anyone who makes you uncomfortable?

SAMPLE DIALOGUE

Talk about what to do if your child reports inappropriate behavior to an adult, only to have it be brushed aside. Discuss options in this scenario like finding another adult or calling someone on his or her trusted adults list.

19.
WHAT TO DO IF SOMETHING HAS HAPPENED TO YOU – WHO TO TALK TO

- A CHILD SHOULD ALWAYS TELL SOMEONE RIGHT AWAY IF HE OR SHE IS EVER TOUCHED IN A WAY THAT MAKES HIM OR HER FEEL UNCOMFORTABLE

- WHO SHOULD YOU TALK TO IF SOMEONE TOUCHES YOU IN THIS WAY?

- TRUSTWORTHY ADULTS CAN INCLUDE DOCTORS, POLICE OFFICERS, AND PARENTS

- NOT EVEN TRUSTED ADULTS SHOULD MAKE YOU FEEL UNCOMFORTABLE

- YOU WON'T BE IN TROUBLE AND YOU WILL BE BELIEVED

20.
HOW PREDATORS GROOM CHILDREN

- WHAT DOES IT MEAN FOR A PREDATOR TO GROOM CHILDREN FOR SEXUAL MOLESTATION/ABUSE?

- PREDATORS ARE OFTEN PEOPLE THE CHILD KNOWS

- LISTEN TO YOUR INSTINCTS

- CHILDREN SHOULD NEVER KEEP SECRETS ABOUT SEX FROM PARENTS

START THE CONVERSATION

Explain to your kids that predators may seek to gain the victim's trust, then start to desensitize the child to physical touch by using innocent, affectionate touch, such as a pat on the back or a squeeze of an arm, first. Predators can sometimes be "friends" or peers, isolate their victims, and seek to fill a void in the child's life. Remind your child that no one has a right to touch him or her without his or her consent, not even relatives or grown-up friends. Talk specifically about your family policies for taking rides, texting or messaging, spending time alone with adults and teens who are not on the "trusted adults list." This is also a good time to talk about online predators who might contact your kids through gaming sites, social media, etc. Emphasize the need to be honest with you about their online behavior and to never speak to strangers online—even if they seem to be other kids.

ADDITIONAL QUESTIONS TO CONSIDER

What are some warning signs we can look for in adults or teens? (progressive, inappropriate touch, privately texting your child, etc.)

What are some ways we can stay safe from online predators?

SAMPLE DIALOGUE

Create a plan with your child. Ask them what they can do if they are at a friend's house and an older kid or adult makes them feel uncomfortable, tries to get them alone, etc. Can they call you and say a "safe word" that your family has agreed on? What else can they do?

For more ideas, see our Lesson on "Teaching Your Child About Predators," available at educateempowerkids.org.

PREDATOR: *A sexual predator is someone who seeks to obtain sexual contact through hunting.*

SURVEY 2 **8–11**

Please reflect on your discussions with your child up to this point and answer the following questions.

1. Select the topic that has been the most difficult to discuss with your child.

   11. Romantic Love
   12. Different Kinds of Families
   13. Gender Roles
   14. Sexual Identification
   15. Ready for a Sexual Relationship
   16. Curiosity
   17. Masturbation
   18. Children Do Not Have Sex
   19. What to Do if Something Has Happened to You – Who to Talk To
   20. How Predators Groom Children

2. Referring to question 1, why was this topic difficult to discuss?

   _____

   _____

3. What have you said that has surprised you or exceeded your expectations of yourself in some way during the recent discussions?

   _____

   _____

4. What have you learned about your child during the recent discussions?

   _____

   _____

If you scan the code below, you can take this survey online. This will help us improve our curriculum and create new resources for parents.

START THE CONVERSATION

Explain when you expect your children to be obedient–for example, when asked to clean a room or pick up dirty clothes. Describe times when they'll need to have the courage to say "NO" to an adult. Discuss different types of dangerous situations your child may encounter: Such as when he or she is made to feel uncomfortable by what someone does or says. Talk about which situations your child can say no in, not just who they can say no to. Practice yelling "NO!"

ADDITIONAL QUESTIONS TO CONSIDER

Ask your child: What can you say or do if someone tries to touch you on the private areas of your body, tries to take your clothes off, or tries to take your picture when you are wearing a bathing suit or less clothes? (Yell NO! and run to a safe adult.)

What are some other circumstances where you can say "No"?

 CONSENT: *Clear agreement or permission to permit something or to do something.*

21.
HOW TO
SAY "NO"

- 🗨 YOU CAN SAY NO TO ANYONE

- 👑 WHEN IS IT VERY IMPORTANT TO SAY NO TO SOMEONE?

- 🗨 PRACTICE SAYING NO LOUDLY AND FIRMLY

- 🗨 EVEN IF YOU HAVE DONE SOMETHING IN THE PAST, IT DOESN'T MEAN YOU HAVE TO DO IT AGAIN

22.
YOU HAVE INSTINCTS THAT KEEP YOU SAFE

- INSTINCTS ARE A PART OF US AND CAN KEEP US SAFE

- INSTINCTS CAN HELP US MAKE GOOD DECISIONS

- HAVE YOU EVER HAD THAT "ICKY" FEELING? WHAT DOES THAT "ICKY" FEELING MEAN?

 **INSTINCT:**

An inherent inclination towards a particular behavior. Behavior that is performed without being based on prior experience is instinctive.

START THE CONVERSATION

Describe a scenario for your child like seeing a big spider or snake or someone jumping out to scare you to describe instincts. Ask your child if he or she has ever had "gut" or instinct feelings, either positive or negative. Talk about how we can be more sensitive to these feelings.

ADDITIONAL QUESTIONS TO CONSIDER

What do instincts feel like?

What are some times or places that our instincts may try to warn us?

SAMPLE SCENARIO

Instincts are similar to an alarm system, that we can feel in a dangerous/uncomfortable situation. It is so important to trust your instincts, don't ignore them just because you don't want to make the person feel bad. Your safety is more important.

23.
PORNOGRAPHY

- WHAT IS PORNOGRAPHY?

- HAVE YOU EVER SEEN PORNOGRAPHY (PORN)?

- PORNOGRAPHY IS DAMAGING TO INDIVIDUALS, RELATIONSHIPS, AND SOCIETY

- DEVELOP A PLAN FOR WHAT TO DO IF YOUR CHILD IS EXPOSED TO PORNOGRAPHY

START THE CONVERSATION

Define pornography and its uses. Explain that it is sometimes used to aid in the sexual abuse of children. Clarify that it is not romantic or at all about love. Describe how it is addictive. Formulate a plan for what to do if your child sees pornography. (Get away from it, find a trusted adult, and tell a parent.) The majority of pornography is now viewed on smart phones and tablets; prepare your child for this probability.

Start by explaining what pornography is: it is pictures or videos of people with little or no clothing. Usually there is sexual behavior in it and it is made for the sole purpose of making money. Ask your child if he or she has ever seen pornography.
Share your personal or family standards about pornography.

Explain that there is nothing wrong with being curious about the human body, that is natural. But pornography is not a healthy way to find answers about the body or sex.

ADDITIONAL QUESTIONS TO CONSIDER

Have you ever seen pornography? What should you do if you see it?

Where are some places you might see porn? (While doing homework, on the school bus, at a friend's house, etc.)

SAMPLE SCENARIO

Try role playing here using a friend with a mobile device as an example and talk about how your child can get away from seeing pornography and who they can talk to about it.

 PORNOGRAPHY: *The portrayal of explicit sexual content for the purpose or intent of causing sexual arousal.*

SEXTING: *The sending or distribution of sexually explicit images, messages, or other material via mobile phones.*

START THE CONVERSATION

Go over your household rules for cell phone and social media use. Consider installing filters and blocks on your computer and child's phone if you have not yet done so. Explain to your kids that a teenager should not get a social media account until they are at least 13 and that many kids' first most porn exposure happens through social media. Discuss what they should do if someone sends them an innapropriate message or sext message. For more information on this, see *Social Media and Teens: The Ultimate Guide for Keeping Kids Safe Online* available on educateempowerkids.org.

ADDITIONAL QUESTIONS TO CONSIDER

What can you do if someone asks your for a nude photo or picture of your breasts or other parts of your body?

Why is it rude or even sexual harrassment to ask someone for a sexually explicit photo?

Why is it unwise to send a naked picture of yourself?

24.
SEXTING AND SOCIAL MEDIA

- WHAT ARE SEXUALLY EXPLICIT MESSAGES?

- EVEN AN INNOCENT RECEIVER OF A NUDE PICTURE CAN GET IN TROUBLE FOR HAVING IT

- PEOPLE HAVE USED SEXTING IMAGES TO GET OTHERS IN TROUBLE

- DISCUSS THE RULES OF YOUR HOUSE FOR USING SOCIAL MEDIA AND CELL PHONES

- WHY DO YOU THINK THESE RULES ARE IMPORTANT?

- WHAT SHOULD YOU DO IF YOU RECEIVE SEXUAL MESSAGES/IMAGES ONLINE OR ON YOUR PHONE?

25.
BEING MEDIA SAVVY

- THE MEDIA CAN INFLUENCE YOUR BODY IMAGE AND THE WAY YOU VIEW SEX

- THE PEOPLE IN MEDIA ARE USUALL PHOTOSHOPPED AND ONLY REPRESENT A VERY NARROW DEFINITION OF BEAUTY

- WE ARE OFTEN EXPOSED TO VERY UNHEALTHY MESSAGES IN MEDIA ABOUT SEX, PEOPLE, LOVE, AND RELATIONSHIPS

START THE CONVERSATION

Teach your child to question the messages he or she sees in all forms of media, especially messages about sex and love. Ask your child if he or she has ever had a negative thought about his or her body. Where did it come from? Talk about ways to counteract what kids see every day. For example: using positive self-talk, knowing the truth about media images, etc. Talk about the fact that commercials are all trying to sell a product and that we should always be looking for the underlying message.

ADDITIONAL QUESTIONS TO CONSIDER

What was the last commercial you saw?

What was it trying to sell?

What did the actress or actor look like?

How were the images in the commercial hyper-sexualized or hyper-masculine?

After considering the ad this way, how does it make you look at commercials differently?

What are some of the messages we see in TV or movies about love, sex, or relationships? Are these healthy or helpful messages?

SAMPLE SCENARIO

Watch a commercial with your child and encourage him or her to deconstruct the images and messages within it.

HYPER-SEXUALIZED: *To make extremely sexual; to accentuate the sexuality of. Often seen in media.*

26.
BODY
IMAGE

- DEVELOPING A HEALTHY BODY IMAGE IMPROVES OUR SELF-WORTH

- HOW DOES BODY IMAGE AFFECT YOUR SENSE OF INHERENT VALUE AS A HUMAN BEING?

- HOW DO YOU SEE YOURSELF?

START THE CONVERSATION

Do not suggest to your child that he or she may become dissatisfied with his or her body. Address body image issues that are present or as they occur in the future with physical development. Discuss keeping oneself healthy. Photoshopped images in the media show impossible standards that no one can attain, not even the people in the images. Refer to chapter 25, Being Media Savvy. Support your child by explaining that while appearance can seem extremely important, in actuality it's a very small part of who we are. Urge your child to realize that he or she decides his or her worth, not the media or mirror. Teach your child that they are worthwhile simply because they exist.

ADDITIONAL QUESTIONS TO CONSIDER

What do you like about the way you look?

How does the way you view your body affect the way you feel about yourself as a whole?

Do you think the people on TV look like the people we know in real life?

Why is being concerned about being a good person more important than worrying about the way we look?

How might our body image affect how we behave in relationships?

 BODY IMAGE:
An individual's feelings regarding their own physical attractiveness and sexuality.

 **SELF-ESTEEM/
SELF-WORTH:** *An
individual's overall
emotional evaluation
of their own worth.*

START THE CONVERSATION

Help your child to understand his or her worth as separate from their appearance. Describe the actions of a person who doesn't feel good about him or herself. (He might be sad, she might tease others, he might hide his body, she might show too much of her body to get attention.) A person with self-respect will carry him or herself with pride and won't do anything intentionally to make others feel uncomfortable. A person who has strong self-worth is confident and is usually kind to others. Ask your child how he or she feels about him or herself. Remind your child that comparing himself to others is unproductive and does not lead to true self-worth.

ADDITIONAL QUESTIONS TO CONSIDER

How might a person who feels good about him or herself act differently from someone who does not?

Where do you find your worth? What qualities do you like about yourself?

How does one's self-worth affect the way he or she treats others?

How might self-worth affect their decision to enter a relationship or have sex?

27.
SELF-WORTH
SELF-ESTEEM

- A PERSON WHO HAS HEALTHY SELF-WORTH BEHAVES DIFFERENTLY FROM SOMEONE WHO DOES NOT

- A PERSON WITH HEALTHY SELF-ESTEEM WILL NOT DO OR ASK OTHERS TO DO THINGS THAT MAKE THEM UNCOMFORTABLE

- THINK ABOUT THE THINGS THAT MAKE YOU UNIQUE

28.
SHAME AND GUILT

- SOME PEOPLE THINK SEX IS BAD OR DIRTY, THIS IS A SAD MYTH

- WHAT SITUATIONS COULD CAUSE SHAME ABOUT SEX?

- SEXUAL ASSAULT CAN CAUSE THE VICTIM TO FEEL SHAME AND GUILT, BUT AN ASSAULT IS NEVER THE VICTIM'S FAULT

START THE CONVERSATION

Sexual intercourse is a very intimate act that often happens naked, which makes people feel vulnerable, sometimes leading to feelings of guilt and shame. Explain the difference between guilt and shame. Guilt can be explained by the notion, "I did something wrong." Shame is more painful and is the idea, "I am a terrible person." Discuss non-consensual sex and sexual assault. Help your child to understand that the perpetrator should feel bad about forcing him or herself on an unwilling person, but any victim should NEVER feel ashamed.

Sex is not bad. It is good and healthy! However, some people feel embarrassed about it, so they make others feel guilty or ashamed about it as well. Sex is a normal, natural act for adults.

ADDITIONAL QUESTIONS TO CONSIDER

What can help you to have a positive attitude about sex?

Do you understand the difference between guilt and shame?

Why do some people feel shameful or guilty about sex?

What can you do if you feel guilty or ashamed about something you have done or seen?

 SHAME: *The painful feeling arising from the consciousness of something dishonorable, improper, ridiculous, etc., done by oneself or another.*

GESTATION: *The time when a person or animal is developing inside its mother before it is born.*

START THE CONVERSATION

Allow your child to ask questions about gestation as you go over the bullet points. During pregnancy, the embryo or fetus grows and develops inside a woman's uterus.

Explain to your child that although sex is usually required for someone to get pregnant, one does not become pregnant every time she has sex.

ADDITIONAL QUESTIONS TO CONSIDER

Let's review topic #7, do you remember how a woman becomes pregnant?

What other physical changes happen to a woman's body during pregnancy?

Do you know how to prevent pregnancy?

29.
PREGNANCY

- SPERM FROM MALE FERTILIZES EGG IN FEMALE

- EGG TRAVELS FROM FALLOPIAN TUBE TO UTERUS

- FERTILIZED EGG IS NOW AN EMBRYO

- A FULL-TERM PREGNANCY LASTS APPROXIMATELY 40 WEEKS

30.
STDs AND STIs

- THERE ARE MANY KINDS OF STDs AND STIs

- PREVENTION INCLUDES ABSTINENCE FOLLOWED BY MONOGAMY, AND REGULAR CONDOM USE

- HOW DOES SOMEONE KNOW IF THEY HAVE AN STI? CAN THEY GET TESTED?

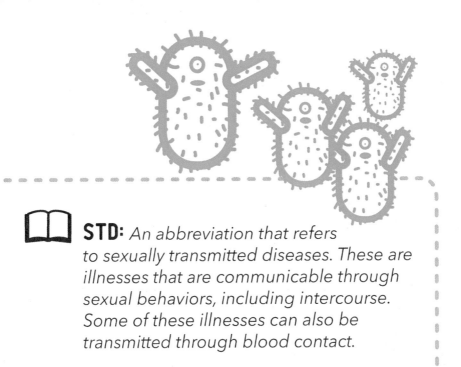

STD: *An abbreviation that refers to sexually transmitted diseases. These are illnesses that are communicable through sexual behaviors, including intercourse. Some of these illnesses can also be transmitted through blood contact.*

START THE CONVERSATION

Ask your child if he has heard of AIDS, HIV, HPV, herpes, syphilis, hepatitis B or C, chlamydia, pubic lice, and/or gonorrhea. Explain that these are all sexually transmitted infections or diseases and that some of them are deadly. (See glossary for definitions.) Others won't kill but will stay in the body for life. Talk about the ways to avoid STIs and STDs: like abstinence and condom use. Many people have begun transitioning from using the term STD to using STI in an effort to clarify that not all sexually transmitted infections turn into a disease. (See the glossary for definitions.)

ADDITIONAL QUESTIONS TO CONSIDER

How are diseases and infections spread? How are STDs and STIs different from colds, flu, warts, lice and other illnesses? These other illnesses are spread through human contact and bodily fluid, but STIs and STDs are transmitted through sexual contact with an infected person.

Thank you for using 30 Days of Sex Talks. Please answer the following questions to help us continue to improve our program.

1. Did you use the sample dialogues and/or activities during your discussions?

   Yes   No

2. Referring to question 1, which dialogues and/or activities worked best and worst for your child?

   Best_____

   Worst_____

3. Please select the topic (if any) that was the most difficult to discuss.

   1. Public versus Private Discussion
   2. Male Anatomy
   3. Female Anatomy
   4. Puberty for Boys
   5. Puberty for Girls
   6. Menstrual Cycle
   7. Physical Mechanics of Sexual Intercourse
   8. Emotional Aspects of Sex
   9. Relationships are Good and Wonderful
   10. What Does a Healthy Relationship Look Like?
   11. Romantic Love
   12. Different Kinds of Families
   13. Gender Roles
   14. Sexual Identification
   15. Ready for a Sexual Relationship
   16. Curiosity
   17. Masturbation
   18. Children Do Not Have Sex

19. What to Do if Something Has Happened to You – Who to Talk To
20. How Predators Groom Children
21. How to Say No
22. You Have Instincts. They Keep You Safe
23. Pornography
24. Sexting and Social Media
25. Being Media Savvy
26. Body Image
27. Self-worth/Self-esteem
28. Shame and Guilt
29. Pregnancy
30. STDs and STIs

4. Referring to question 3, why was this topic difficult to discuss?

_____

_____

5. Having completed this program, please rate your current comfort level of discussing human sexuality with your child.

1   2   3   4   5   6   7   8   9   10

Low   Medium   High

6. Do you feel that your ability to discuss difficult things with your child has been enhanced by these discussions? Please explain your answer.

Yes   No

_____

_____

7. Was there anything that you learned from your child that surprised you (good or bad)? Please describe below.

_____

_____

8. Do you feel that this experience has increased the likelihood of your child coming to you with questions about sex and sexuality?

Yes   No

9. Rate the effectiveness of the overall program below.

1   2   3   4   5   6   7   8   9   10

Low   Medium   High

10. Would you recommend this program to your friends and family?

Yes   No

11. Is there anything that you think the program needs to improve, add, or remove? If so, please explain.

If you scan the code below, you can take this survey online. This will help us improve our curriculum and create new resources for parents.

FREE DOWNLOADABLE!

This curriculum works best when it is interactive between you and your child. To help facilitate this interaction, we've developed topic cards as a companion to this book. The topic cards are a bonus for you to download at your convenience. They can be printed and placed on the refrigerator, on a mirror, in your pocket or wherever they need to be to serve as a reminder to both you and your child to **start talking!**

To obtain your free download, please scan the QR code below and enter the following password: 1qazXSW@

IF YOU ENJOYED THIS BOOK, PLEASE LEAVE A POSITIVE REVIEW ON AMAZON.COM

For great resources and information, follow us on our social media outlets:

Facebook: www.facebook.com/educateempowerkids/
Twitter: @EduEmpowerKids
Pinterest: pinterest.com/educateempower/
Instagram: Eduempowerkids

Subscribe to our website for exclusive offers and information at:
www.educateempowerkids.org

REFERENCES AND RESOURCES

Strengthening your child
30 Days to a Stronger Child

Talking to kids about pornography
How to Talk to Your Kids About Pornography

Hilton, D., & Watts, C. (2011, February 21). Pornography addiction: A neuroscience perspective. Retrieved from http://www. ncbi.nlm.nih.gov/pmc/articles/PMC3050060/

Layden, M. (n.d.). Pornography and Violence: A New Look at Research. Retrieved from http://www.socialcostsofpornography. com/Layden_Pornography_and_Violence.pdf

Voon, V. et. al. (2014, July 11). Neural Correlates of Sexual Cue Reactivity in Individuals with and without Compulsive Sexual Behaviours. Retrieved from http://www.plosone.org/article/info%3Adoi%2F10.1371%2Fjournal.pone.0102419

Rape culture resource
http://www.marshall.edu/wcenter/sexual-assault/rape-culture/

Predator-victim grooming resource
http://www.parenting.org/article/victim-grooming-protect-your-child-from-sexual-predators

Slut-shaming study
http://america.aljazeera.com/articles/2014/5/29/slut-shaming-study.html

Birth control resource
https://www.mayoclinic.org/healthy-lifestyle/birth-control/basics/birth-control-basics/hlv-20049454?reDate=15122018

Pregnancy rates
https://www.hhs.gov/ash/oah/adolescent-development/reproductive-health-and-teen-pregnancy/teen-pregnancy-and-childbearing/trends/index.html#.VBy66hB0ypo

Pregnancy resource
http://www.whattoexpect.com/

STD/STI resource
https://www.womenshealth.gov/a-z-topics/sexually-transmitted-infections

STD/STI rates
http://www.cdc.gov/std/stats/STI-Estimates-Fact-Sheet-Feb-2013.pdf

Domestic violence resource
https://www.justice.gov/ovw/domestic-violence

Domestic violence resource
http://www.thehotline.org/

Information on masturbation and porn use
http://blogs.psychcentral.com/sex/2011/04/compulsive-masturbation-and-porn/

Creating a family media standard
http://bit.ly/1xwb1ri

Lesson on Media Literacy
https://educateempowerkids.org/lesson-media-literacy

Videos related to the 30 Days of Sex Talks books
http://bit.ly/29zyVNW

Social Media and Kids: The Ultimate Guide to Keeping Kids Safe Online
http://bit.ly/2kPS59m

Lesson On Predators
http://bit.ly/1NZVyug

Lesson on Consent
http://bit.ly/2ygwL4e

GLOSSARY

The following terms have been included to assist you as you prepare and hold discussions with your children regarding healthy sexuality and intimacy. The definitions are not intended for the child; rather, they are meant to clarify the concepts and terms for the adult. Some terms may not be appropriate for your child, given their age, circumstances, or your own family culture and values. Use your judgment to determine which terminology best meets your individual needs.

Abstinence: The practice of not doing or having something that is wanted or enjoyable: the practice of abstaining from something.

Abuse: The improper usage or treatment of another person or entity, often to unfairly gain power or other benefit in the relationship.

Affection: A feeling or type of love that exceeds general goodwill.

AIDS: A sexually transmitted or bloodborne viral infection that causes immune deficiency.

Anal Sex: A form of intercourse that generally involves the insertion and thrusting of the erect penis into the anus or rectum for sexual pleasure.

Anus: The external opening of the rectum comprised of two sphincters which control the exit of feces from the body.

Appropriate: Suitable, proper, or fitting for a particular purpose, person, or circumstance.

Arousal: The physical and emotional response to sexual desire during or in anticipation of sexual activity.

Bisexual: Sexual orientation in which one is attracted to both males and females.

Body Image: An individual's feelings regarding their own physical attractiveness and sexuality. These feelings and opinions are often influenced by other people and media sources.

Bodily Integrity: The personal belief that our bodies, while crucial to our understanding of who we are, do not in themselves solely define our worth; the knowledge that our bodies are the storehouse of our humanity; and the sense that we esteem our bodies and we treat them accordingly.

Boundaries: The personal limits or guidelines that an individual forms in order to clearly identify what are reasonable and safe behaviors for others to engage in around him or her.

Bowel Movement: Also known as defecation, a bowel movement is the final act of digestion by which waste is eliminated from the body via the anus.

Breasts: Women develop breasts on their upper torso during puberty. Breasts contain mammary glands, which create the breast milk used to feed infants.

Child: A person between birth and full growth.

Chlamydia: Bacteria that causes or is associated with various diseases of the eye and urogenital tract.

Clitoris: A female sex organ visible at the front juncture of the labia minora above the opening of the urethra. The clitoris is the female's most sensitive erogenous zone.

Condom: A thin rubber covering that a man wears on his penis during sex in order to prevent a woman from becoming pregnant or to prevent the spread of diseases.

Consent: Clear agreement or permission to permit something or to do something. Consent must be given freely, without force or intimidation, and while the person is fully conscious and cognizant of their present situation.

Contraceptive: A method, device, or medication that works to prevent pregnancy. Another name for birth control.

Curiosity: The desire to learn or know more about something or someone.

Date Rape: A rape in which the perpetrator has a relationship that is, to some degree, either romantic or potentially sexual with the victim. The perpetrator uses physical force, psychological intimidation, or drugs or alcohol to force the victim to have sex either against their will or in a state in which they cannot give clear consent.

Degrade: To treat with contempt or disrespect.

Demean: To cause a severe loss in the dignity of or respect for another person.

Derogatory: An adjective that implies severe criticism or loss of respect.

Diaphragm: A cervical barrier type of birth control made of a soft latex or silicone dome with a spring molded into the rim. The spring creates a seal against the walls of the vagina, preventing semen, including sperm, from entering the fallopian tubes.

Domestic Abuse/Domestic Violence: A pattern of abusive behavior in any relationship that is used by one partner to gain or maintain power and control over another intimate partner. It can be physical, sexual, emotional, economic, or psychological actions or threats of actions that influence another person. (DOJ definition)

Double Standard: A rule or standard that is applied differently and unfairly to a person or distinct groups of people.

Egg Cell: The female reproductive cell, which, when fertilized by sperm inside the uterus, will eventually grow into an infant.

Ejaculation: When a man reaches orgasm, during which semen is expelled from the penis.

Emotional Abuse: A form of abuse in which another person is subjected to behavior that can result in psychological trauma. Emotional abuse often occurs within relationships in which there is a power imbalance.

Emotional Intimacy: As aspect of relationships that is dependent upon trust and that can be expressed both verbally and non-verbally. Emotional intimacy displays a degree of closeness that exceeds that normally experienced in common relational interactions.

Epididymal Hypertension: A condition that results from prolonged sexual arousal in human males in which fluid congestion in the testicles occurs, often accompanied by testicular pain. The condition is temporary. Also referred to as "blue balls."

Erection: During a penile erection, the penis becomes engorged and enlarged due to the dilation of the cavernosal arteries (which run the length of the penis) and subsequent engorgement of the surrounding corporal tissue with blood.

Explicit: An adjective signifying that something is stated clearly, without room for confusion or doubt. Sexually explicit material, however, signifies that the content contains sexual material that may be considered offensive or overtly graphic.

Extortion: To obtain something through force or via threats.

Family: A group consisting of parents and children living together in a household. The definition of family is constantly evolving, and every person can define family in a different way to encompass the relationships he or she shares with people in his or her life. Over time one's family will change as one's life changes and the importance of family values and rituals deepen.

Female Arousal: The physiological responses to sexual desire during or in anticipation of sexual activity in women include vaginal lubrication (wetness), engorgement of the external genitals (clitoris and labia), enlargement of the vagina, and dilation of the pupils.

Fertilize: The successful union between an egg (technically known as the ovum) and a sperm, which normally occurs within the second portion of the fallopian tube (known as the ampulla). The result of fertilization is a zygote (fertilized egg).

Friend: Someone with whom a person has a relationship of mutual affection. A friend is closer than an associate or acquaintance. Friends typically share emotions and characteristics such as affection, empathy, honesty, trust, and compassion.

Gay: A word used to describe people who are sexually attracted to members of the same sex. The term "lesbian" is generally preferred when talking about women who are attracted to other women. Originally, the word "gay" meant "carefree"; its connection to sexual orientation developed during the latter half of the 20th century.

Gender: Masculinity and femininity are differentiated through a range of characteristics known as "gender." They may include biological sex (being male or female), social roles based upon biological sex, and one's subjective experience and understanding of their own gender identity.

Gender Role: The pattern of masculine or feminine behavior of an individual that is defined by a particular culture and that is largely determined by a child's upbringing.

Gender Stereotypes: A thought or understanding applied to either males or females (or other gender identities) that may or may not correspond with reality. "Men don't cry" or "women are weak" are examples of inaccurate gender stereotypes.

Gestation: The time when a person or animal is developing inside its mother before it is born.

Gonorrhea: A contagious inflammation of the genital mucous membrane caused by the gonococcus.

Groom: To prepare or train someone for a particular purpose or activity. In the case of sexual predators, it is any willful action made by the offender to prepare the victim and/or the victim's support network that allows for easier sex offending.

Healthy Sexuality: Having the ability to express one's sexuality in ways that contribute positively to one's own self-esteem and relationships. Healthy sexuality includes approaching sexual relationships and interactions with mutual agreement and dignity. It necessarily includes mutual respect and a lack of fear, shame, or guilt, and never includes coercion or violence.

Hepatitis B: A sometimes fatal disease caused by a double-stranded DNA virus that tends to persist in the blood serum and is transmitted especially by contact with infected blood (as by transfusion or by sharing contaminated needles in illicit intravenous drug use) or by contact with other infected bodily fluids such as semen.

Hepatitis C: Caused by a single-stranded RNA virus of the family Flaviviridae that tends to persist in the blood serum and is usually transmitted by infected blood (as by injection of an illicit drug, blood transfusion, or exposure to blood or blood products).

Herpes: Any of several inflammatory diseases of the skin caused by herpes viruses and characterized by clusters of vesicles.

Heterosexual: Sexual orientation in which one is attracted to members of the opposite sex (males are attracted to females; females are attracted to males).

HIV: Any of several retroviruses and especially HIV-1 that infect and destroy helper T cells of the immune system causing the marked reduction in their numbers that is diagnostic of AIDS.

Homosexual: Sexual orientation in which one is attracted to members of the same sex (males are attracted to males; females are attracted to females).

Hook up Sex: A form of casual sex in which sexual activity takes place outside the context of a committed relationship. The sex may be a one-time event, or an ongoing arrangement; in either case, the focus is generally on the physical enjoyment of sexual activity without an emotional involvement or commitment.

HPV: Human papillomavirus.

Hymen: A membrane that partially closes the opening of the vagina and whose presence is traditionally taken to be a mark of virginity. However, it can often be broken before a woman has sex simply by being active, and sometimes it is not present at all.

Hyper-sexualized: To make extremely sexual; to accentuate the sexuality of. Often seen in media.

Instinct: An inherent inclination towards a particular behavior. Behavior that is performed without being based on prior experience is instinctive.

Intercourse: Sexual activity, also known as coitus or copulation, which is most commonly understood to refer to the insertion of the penis into the vagina (vaginal sex). It should be noted that there are a wide range of various sexual activities and the boundaries of what constitutes sexual intercourse are still under debate.

Intimacy: Generally a feeling or form of significant closeness. There are four types of intimacy: physical intimacy (sensual proximity or touching), emotional intimacy (close connection resulting from trust and love), cognitive or intellectual intimacy (resulting from honest exchange of thoughts and ideas), and experiential intimacy (a connection that occurs while acting together). Emotional and physical intimacy are often associated with sexual relationships, while intellectual and experiential intimacy are not.

Labia: The inner and outer folds of the vulva on both sides of the vagina.

Lesbian: A word used to describe women who are sexually attracted to other women.

Lice (Pubic): A sucking louse infesting the pubic region of the human body.

Love: A wide range of emotional interpersonal connections, feelings, and attitudes. Common forms include kinship or familial love, friendship, divine love (as demonstrated through worship), and sexual or romantic love. In biological terms, love is the attraction and bonding that functions to unite human beings and facilitate the social and sexual continuation of the species.

Masturbation: The self-stimulation of the genitals in order to produce sexual arousal, pleasure, and orgasm.

Media Literacy: The ability to study, understand, and create messages in various media such as books, social media posts, and photos, movies, games, music, news stories, online ads, blog posts, school essays, etc.

Menstrual Cycle: Egg is released from ovaries through fallopian tube into uterus. Each month, blood and tissue build up in the uterus. When the egg is not fertilized, this blood and tissue are not needed and are shed from the body through the vagina. Cycle is roughly 28 days but can vary. Bleeding time lasts from 2-7 days. May be accompanied by cramping, breast tenderness, and emotional sensitivity.

Menstrual Period: A discharging of blood, secretions, and tissue debris from the uterus at periods of approximately one month in females of breeding age that are not pregnant.

Misogyny: The hatred, aversion, hostility, or dislike of women or girls. Misogyny can appear in a single individual, or may also be manifest in broad cultural trends that undermine women's autonomy and value.

Monogamy: A relationship in which a person has one partner at any one time.

Nipples: The circular, somewhat conical structure of tissue on the breast. The skin of the nipple and its surrounding areola are often several shades darker than that of the surrounding breast tissue. In women, the nipple delivers breast milk to infants.

Nocturnal Emissions A spontaneous orgasm that occurs during sleep. Nocturnal emissions can occur in both males (ejaculation) and females (lubrication of the vagina). The term "wet dream" is often used to describe male nocturnal emissions.

Nudity: The state of not wearing any clothing. Full nudity denotes a complete absence of clothing, while partial nudity is a more ambiguous term, denoting the presence of an indeterminate amount of clothing.

Oral Sex: Sexual activity that involves stimulation of the genitals through the use of another person's mouth.

Orgasm: The rhythmic muscular contractions in the pelvic region that occur as a result of sexual stimulation, arousal, and activity during the sexual response cycle. Orgasms are characterized by a sudden release of built-up sexual tension and by the resulting sexual pleasure.

Penis: The external male sexual organ comprised of the shaft, foreskin, glans penis, and meatus. The penis contains the urethra, through which both urine and semen travel to exit the body.

Perception: A way of regarding, understanding, or interpreting something; a mental impression

Period: The beginning of the menstrual cycle.

Physical Abuse: The improper physical treatment of another person or entity designed to cause bodily harm, pain, injury, or other suffering. Physical abuse is often employed to unfairly gain power or other benefit in the relationship.

The Pill: An oral contraceptive for women containing the hormones estrogen and progesterone or progesterone alone, that inhibits ovulation, fertilization, or implantation of a fertilized ovum, causing temporary infertility. Common brands include Ortho Tri-Cyclen, Yasmin, and Ortho-Novum.

Pornography: The portrayal of explicit sexual content for the purpose or intent of causing sexual arousal. In it, sex and bodies are commodified for the purpose of making a financial profit. It can be created in a variety of media contexts, including videos, photos, animation, books and magazines. Its most lucrative means of distribution is though the internet. The industry that creates pornography is a sophisticated, corporatized, billion dollar business.

Positive Self-Talk: Anything said to oneself for encouragement or motivation, such as phrases or mantras; also, one's ongoing internal conversation with oneself, like a running commentary, which influences how one feels and behaves.

Predator: A predator is technically an organism or being that hunts and then feeds on their prey. A sexual predator is someone who seeks to obtain sexual contact through "hunting." The term is often used to describe the deceptive and coercive methods used by people who commit sex crimes where there is a victim, such as rape or child abuse.

Pregnancy: The common term used for gestation in humans. During pregnancy, the embryo or fetus grows and develops inside a woman's uterus.

Premature Ejaculation: When a man regularly reaches orgasm, during which semen is expelled from the penis, prior to or within one minute of the initiation of sexual activity.

Priapism: The technical term of a condition in which the erect penis does not return to flaccidity within four hours, despite the absence of physical or psychological sexual stimulation.

Private: Belonging to or for the use of a specific individual. Private and privacy denote a state of being alone, solitary, individual, exclusive, secret, personal, hidden, and confidential.

Psychological Abuse: A form of abuse in which a person is subjected to behavior that can result in psychological trauma. Psychological abuse often occurs within relationships in which there is a power imbalance.

Puberty: A period or process through which children reach sexual maturity. Once a person has reached puberty, their body is capable of sexual reproduction.

Public: Belonging to or for the use of all people in a specific area, or all people as a whole. Something that is public is common, shared, collective, communal, and widespread.

Rape: A sex crime in which the perpetrator forces another person to have sexual intercourse against their will and without consent. Rape often occurs through the threat or actuality of violence against the victim.

Rape Culture: A culture in which rape is pervasive and to an extent normalized due to cultural and societal attitudes towards gender and sexuality. Behaviors that facilitate rape culture include victim blaming, sexual objectification, and denial regarding sexual violence.

Relationship: The state of being connected, united, or related to another person.

Rhythm Method: A method of avoiding pregnancy by restricting sexual intercourse to the times of a woman's menstrual cycle when ovulation and conception are least likely to occur. Because it can be difficult to predict ovulation and because abstinence has to be practiced for up to ten days of a woman's cycle, the effectiveness of the rhythm method is on average just 75-87%, according to http://www.webmd.com.

Romantic Love: A form of love that denotes intimacy and a strong desire for emotional connection with another person to whom one is generally also sexually attracted.

Scrotum: The pouch of skin underneath the penis that contains the testicles.

Self-Esteem / Self -Worth: An individual's overall emotional evaluation of their own worth. Self-esteem is both a judgment of the self and an attitude toward the self. More generally, the term is used to describe a confidence in one's own value or abilities.

Semen: The male reproductive fluid, which contains spermatozoa in suspension. Semen exits the penis through ejaculation.

Serial Monogamy: A mating system in which a man or woman can only form a long-term, committed relationship (such as marriage) with one partner at a time. Should the relationship dissolve, the individual may go on to form another relationship, but only after the first relationship has ceased.

Sexting: The sending or distribution of sexually explicit images, messages, or other material via mobile phones.

Sexual Abuse: The improper sexual usage or treatment of another person or entity, often to unfairly gain power or other benefit in the relationship. In instances of sexual abuse, undesired sexual behaviors are forced upon one person by another.

Sexual Assault: A term often used in legal contexts to refer to sexual violence. Sexual assault occurs when there is any non-consensual sexual contact or violence. Examples include rape, groping, forced kissing, child sexual abuse, and sexual torture.

Sexual Harassment: Harassment involving unwanted sexual advances or obscene remarks. Sexual harassment can be a form of sexual coercion as well as an undesired sexual proposition, including the promise of reward in exchange for sexual favors.

Sexual Identification: How one thinks of oneself in terms of whom one is romantically or sexually attracted to.

Sexual Molestation: Aggressive and persistent harassment, either psychological or physical, of a sexual manner.

Shame: The painful feeling arising from the consciousness of something dishonorable, improper, ridiculous, etc., done by oneself or another.

Slut-shaming: The act of criticizing, attacking, or shaming a woman for her real or presumed sexual activity, or for behaving in ways that someone thinks are associated with her real or presumed sexual activity.

Sperm: The male reproductive cell, consisting of a head, midpiece, and tail. The head contains the genetic material, while the tail is used to propel the sperm as it travels towards the egg.

Spontaneous Erection: A penile erection that occurs as an automatic response to a variety of stimuli, some of which is sexual and some of which is physiological.

STD: An abbreviation that refers to sexually transmitted diseases. These are illnesses that are communicable through sexual behaviors, including intercourse. Some of these illnesses can also be transmitted through blood contact.

STI: An abbreviation that refers to sexually transmitted infections. These are illnesses that are communicable through sexual behaviors, including intercourse. Some of these illnesses can also be transmitted through blood contact. Not all STI's lead to a disease and become an STD.

Straight: A slang term for heterosexuality, a sexual orientation in which one is attracted to members of the opposite sex (males are attracted to females; females are attracted to males).

Syphilis: A chronic, contagious, usually venereal and often congenital, disease caused by a spirochete, and if left untreated, producing chancres, rashes, and systemic lesions in a clinical course with three stages continued over many years.

Test Touch: Seemingly innocent touches by a predator or offender, such as a pat on the back or a squeeze on the arm, that are meant to normalize kids to being in physical contact with the predator. Test touches can progress to trying to be alone with the child.

Testicles: The male gonad, which is located inside the scrotum beneath the penis. The testicles are responsible for the production of sperm and androgens, primarily testosterone.

Transgender: A condition or state in which one's physical sex does not match one's gender identity. A transgender individual may have been assigned a sex at birth based on their genitals, but feel that this assignation is false or incomplete. They also may be someone who does not conform to conventional gender roles but instead combines or moves between them.

Uncomfortable: Feeling or causing discomfort or unease; disquieting.

Under the Influence: Being physically affected by alcohol or drugs

Urethra: The tube that connects the urinary bladder to the urinary meatus (the orifice through which the urine exits the urethra tube). In males, the urethra runs down the penis and opens at the end of the penis. In females, the urethra is internal and opens between the clitoris and the vagina.

Urination: The process through which urine is released from the urinary bladder to travel down the urethra and exit the body at the urinary meatus.

Uterus: A major reproductive sex organ in the female body. The uterus is located in the lower half of the torso, just above the vagina. It is the site in which offspring are conceived and in which they gestate during the term of the pregnancy.

Vagina: The muscular tube leading from the external genitals to the cervix of the uterus in women. During sexual intercourse, the penis can be inserted into the vagina. During childbirth, the infant exits the uterus through the vagina.

Vaginal Sex: A form of sexual intercourse in which the penis is inserted into the vagina.

Vaginismus: A medical condition in which a woman is unable to engage in any form of vaginal penetration, including sexual intercourse, the use of tampons or menstrual cups, and that of gynecological examinations, due to involuntary pain.

Victim: A person who is harmed, injured, or killed as the result of an accident or crime.

Virgin: A male or female who has never engaged in sexual intercourse.

Vulva: The parts of the female sexual organs that are on the outside of the body.

Wet Dreams : A slang term for nocturnal emissions. A nocturnal emission is a spontaneous orgasm that occurs during sleep. Nocturnal emissions can occur in both males (ejaculation) and females (lubrication of the vagina).

Made in the USA
Monee, IL
20 March 2023